SWANSO

C000152057

Sue Lenier

SWANSONGS

Sue Lenier

The Oleander Press

OLEANDER MODERN POETS XII

The Oleander Press
17 Stansgate Avenue
Cambridge CB2 2QZ, England

The Oleander Press
210 Fifth Avenue
New York, N.Y. 10010, U.S.A.

2nd impression 1982
3 rd impression 1982

British Library Cataloguing in Publication Data

Lenier, Susan Jennifer
   Swansongs.—(Oleander modern poets; 12)
   I. Title II. Series
   821'.914   PR6062.E/

   ISBN 0-906672-04-X
        0-906672-03-1 Pbk

ACKNOWLEDGMENTS
We greatly appreciate permission received to
reprint Sue Lenier's poems from the Royal College
of Art (for the works in *Once Off*, 1980),
from *Collaborations* (York, 1980), and from
Magnet (Warwick, 1981).
Cover design by Harry Weinberger.

Text design by Ron Jones

Printed and bound in Great Britain

SUE LENIER

Sue Lenier was born in Birmingham in 1957, went to school on Tyneside, and won a place at Cambridge University in 1977, graduating in 1980. After this she spent a year, sponsored by industry, writing and performing in England and Germany, and is currently (1981–3) on a Harkness Fellowship in the United States. Asked about her aims as a poet, she has said:

"My primary aim is to create something that is beautiful and, as far as I can judge it, accurate. This never changes. What does change are the means by which I imagine I can accomplish this. There are, however, even in these means, certain constant obsessions—colour, light and rhythms fascinate me. Particularly violent dramatic changes of these—I like the 'wandering along' feel of a sonnet, but also vicious changes in rhythm and rhyme like in 'The Blind Minotaur'. The moment when all becomes dark or grows light, when all possibilities of change are there, is endlessly obsessive. It is, always, the theatre that I can find in poetry that I end up returning to. The potential for creating a scene in language, and giving each word and image an unstated emotive value. When I write 'nature' poetry, I'm writing about theatre not nature, conflicts and violence and sudden beauty. I'm not interested in nature except as a vehicle for emotional drama.

"Moods and rhythms tend to be quick, like the imagery—I prefer movement to repose in poetry, and emotional action to contemplation.

"As for how it has changed and will change?—I don't know. I'm moving away from stylised language to freer prosier work and from pretty, direct imagery to uglier and more indirect. That's all I can tell at the moment."

Sue Lenier has also written a number of plays.

CONTENTS

Your kisses peck me like birds
And lightly scatter like birds, in a wind
Yet their nip and their sweet song
Leave me silent, through storms.

Light, blackblossomed and bare,
Shines slight and far away on the stretching hills
And curves inwards into cherry-red bites
That linger and pinch in winter nails
At the supple white flesh. Your eyes are far
And blown as crow wings, scuttling, shatterfeathered
And light-beaked blown through the swirling swinging air —
My breasts are still and touched and prick with red and run
In stripping falling whiteness, soft and strewn,
They gently puff in snow around your forcing passionate bending
                                                        /head.

Mourn no more for the flowers you have broken,
Lies you have told and clouds stirred on my face
Roused from my dark to the moons you have awoken,
In this fair night your blackness keeps no place,
When Winter holds her blue tongue to the trees
Licking them white, they cry not at their death
With tears like wings of flies washed in the breeze
And blown away, each sad and lonely breath,
And as each creature waits for Spring's pale arms
To rouse their sleep and tenderly lead them out,
So I to you who did me all this harm
Will wait, heart-full, to wake you with my shout
    Of happiness, love and trembling sin —
    As all the night goes out, the stars come in.

HILLS AND TREES IN WINTER ▽

The quiet faces of snowflakes reach out to nod and kiss me with
/desire
Of a deadening frozen country. Hard, in the North,
Prick hills like standing icicles, tree-scooped and cold,
Stately as a mushroom in a storm.
The snow stomps and plods in graceful gravity
Over the swelling bruises of hills—deer graze lightly,
Squirrels leap and the air is hard and lovely
Fast-asleep as bears in the West.
I saw them play once, hugging a tight fir-cone,
And loving they garnished the trees decorate with black fur,
Arms, wide-clawed and spread in kindly halter, round its neck,
They slid and clambered above the mushroomed hills
Standing white in a storm.

▽

Silver leaves in shuddering outlines twist their face
To earth-beaten soil, in alien sullen gaze
Beating their bodies in wrenches of silver lace
Faint traced by black hands hidden in the blaze
Of sudden wintry, frost-driven icicle cones
Leaking from the trees, falling from roofs
And ranting through the animals' cold numbed bones
That slash and sliver sharply through the grooves;
Yellow leaves, green and withered fingers
Hard, nails-cracked against the staining glass
Carved in sweet ice, curved in delicate wingers
Along each tripping nail's attempt to pass
    And restore to itself in glorious vision
    The winter's seed that mocks itself in derision.

As icicles walk their wintry way across
The rims of scattered parks and trees
And shining fast their lives of brief bitter loss
Speak of the deaths of Winter who will seize
In blue clenched hand the petals of the flowers
And clench them into silver stiffened fists
That curdle creep more solidly each hour
And tremble as the ice licks their green wrist,
As Winter bullies travellers setting forth
With flaming mouths and covered chequered coat,
The shadows lie and slink out from the north
With dark blindfolds to wrap round every throat
    And silver glittered scarves that harvest call
    And snicker as they make the traveller fall.

The flowers are mad tonight, my love —
Wild and white-petalled, they sing sweetly
Under the blossoms' still, pale arm,
But I feel them come closer to us still
With wild fragrant breaths of poison and harm;

Ah love, my love, pick flowers from a garden
And come, murderous one, in your shroud,
And ravished, ask for pardon.

Love lines the waiting streets with green
Long as limes and bending cool through still air,
Flowers weep and wounded in the cool soil
We lie, soft as shredded silver mice,
Long-tailed, oh, you, my love and I.

Sweet dear, dear sweet, run and pick flowers,
My murderous one, breasts pale as corn
And cunt-wet, you, my sane,
Run trickling and wet to me, with your presents from the rain.

Oh madness and love, together, my love,
And flowers strewn with love and tears and rain
  The faintness of any sign
  The paleness is mine
And these petals, hoped with blood, are white, love, with pains,
/yours and mine.

▽

Crystal trees shiver in the early morning. Decked with frost
And lit they shine like candles down a lazy avenue and I move
Near lacy and kiss you, the stars' pale black fingers cut my throat
In diamonds gaping in the sky, a white branch stung with birds
As Summer's pale lacy neck stretches like a cream cone
Through the night and drips her pale cold fingers lying by
And near to us in starry anemones, melting snowdrops,
Heat-driven into Spring and greens that rise like lawnmowers
Cut off, half starved, cocks riding cockhorse, high —
Oh this light that pierces me like needles with love for you
Trailing in forgotten white wistful cotton from the knees of the
/girdled sky.

▽

Rainbuds sparkling on the ground
Splash over the tumbling nerves of snowdrops,
Pale and wilful they droop and shudder
Cold maids under the colder ground.

▽

The mourning swallows flicking black and white
Through staining clouds, all torn with sunlight's weather
Tottering bright and bold, sing as they lose their flight
Then climb in silky gold on every feather
Back to their thrones that announce the gay springtime
Has come with orange headdress, tufted greens
That squirrel-like spring out and dance behind
The fresh blink of the crocuses' watery dreams

12

In paddling strokes of slimmer emerald line
That lie like wires against the chequered glow
Of Dawn's bright slippers' shadows trembling fire
And lapping off the shadows where they go,
      So early age will run and rise in cold
      As icing tips the lambs from out the fold.

—————————————————————————————————— ▽

Brilliant in star-passioned gapes comes the sun
Chequered in fantastic yellows and rising
In a blur-faced glow through the bloody lands
That wait white-faced, impassioned for the light,
And rising sways, and coming falls
And green leaves bitter tumble through the spring
In brandy flavours, petal-flowered and low
And calling against the love-strewn grass
Who cries and sobs and brilliant dew-lined fogs
In the early smiles of grey-toothed dawn,
And sings like a bird as larks rise
Smooth and wing-edged, grey-smiled through
The rusty beckoning dawn.

—————————————————————————————————— ▽

You, slender and pure as a flame,
You, as the morning, charming and light,
As white as blooming rice from glowing stalks,
You as secret and shining as any dream's source.

Oh carry me off on sunny mats,
Meet me in the afternoon's shadows,
Oh flicker my life, my way in shadows,
Your braising blowing wind from cold shoulders.

You are my love and my thankful desire,
I breathe you in with every slice of air,
You slender and pale as any flame,
You slender and bright as any morning.

The yellow dripping wraiths of splendid rain
Hood and lower in weakening prey around us,
Glittering windows, icicle-bared and bound and stark,
Stand hasty in the mournful early light
And weep beneath the shadow. A sun, apple-green,
Contented as a summer ball, kicks running at the
Sly asides of smirking winds. Birds snicker in the trees
And children run like maddened hens through dust
Chased by the sticking cold. A worm lies dead and long
And single between a gold band of hair-torn sunlight,
Caught and swinging between the ruffled white-edged eyes of trees.

LES FLEURS DU MAL ▽

The flowers of evil desert into dust,
The flowers of red fall mad,
The flowers of silver switch from harsh lust
And the flowers of corruption we had,

And evil scattered away
From these lands of white and blue,
Away from me, away from you,
And the ancient vows that we held to be true
Were lost in the lies of the day.

Oh dust and evil, douleur and hate,
I feel the rats walk wrinkling by,
I see the stars fall wrinkling down
And I watch the flowers in your eye.

Gold-breasted, long-armed I saw you journeying soon
And heard you soon, in gypsy flowers
The wandering rose and smoothly ice-tailed shark
Hang in mats of milk from your tender harsh breasts.

Among these chariots flared with invisible arms
All life is blotted under the sleepy druglifted sky,
All life in the mournful regrets of life that is sadly wandering by.

From the bottom of sandy grills,
I have seen the world spinning like a peacock,
Her tail is loosed in stars,
Her eyes in earthly fires.

Blossom the rocks, flower out the desert
Into a blue and watchful gaze
Traced from the sky who gave,
Returned from the sky who saves.

▽

Pulsing apricots wreck red through the Spring
In flares of orange and green and spread the bark
With luscious fruit-rich cries that hang and dim
Within the white-toothed setting of the dark
And as their richness swells and clusters farther
Amongst the trees whose green hands greedy yank
Against the stubborn earth who'd subtler rather
Throw up white lilies than these feastlings rank
Of brilliant startled orange in the sun
That sleeps and glitters, coma'd by their look
Of faint fresh virgin rippling as they tongue
The sleepy branches toiling in the crook
    Of elbows clinging joyless to the bark
    And greedy reaching to the glittering dark.

Bears dinking through the black night,
Birds singing yelling to the far-out breeze,
Grooving in a lonely hole, its skirt too tight
Hid flies out, splits, drops down its knees.

Spring is here, waving her silver horn
And old black trumpet through the wood,
Her hair fresh-permed, her wide white eyes,
And lashed with pinkish flowers, sprouting in a flood.

Life laughs and dances, night sings,
Day shouts and jumps and falls down the hole,
Rock, oh boy, until time rings loudly
Offkey, flat it wakes sweet Summer's soul.

▽

Huge pink tassels of embroidered light
Lay sharp against the sky and wept
As Dawn tousle-haired and jealous ran blue-jeaned up
And wide-eyed back and out to streak
In brilliant orange-yellows, casual and sandal-less out;
Oh summer, sweet as wooing still air
And pale as breath overburdened with delicate fragrance,
Do not wait for the silent sparkling rain
To tread barefoot and heavy through the clouds,
Do not wish for the eager crying birds
To drag you screaming and unready back.

▽

Poetry lifts my arm and swings it like a swan's wing,
Loose, untied forever,
Nothing ever lost nor ever beautiful
Can help lying falling together.

I remember days wet with thistleseed
Yet sweet as summer honey, where we plucked
Ourselves from the dark damp grass
Throwing a table of dry purple flowers
Eating up bindweeds—stardust and thistles
Rule through throats and mouths
Too long, too gone from kissing,
Oh how I remember you
Dancing white and freely light
Above the scuttling trembling spiders —
Here am I caught and flaked,
Forgotten and forever, lost and widowed
Sitting, spinning a web through red nights
Caught...caught...

Snatch in the teeth of a better light —

Lovely as a garden sprung with flowers
Where lilies shake and leaves spread with the moon,
Oh come love, aching love, and laugh
Before me like the ghost who soon
And transparent floats in silent eyeawakened dreams,
Oh nothing is that is, nothing seems that seems.

Pale and starcoloured in the empty belief
Of possible Universes lifting in the night
And left to hang...

His voice is like bells, like bells...
Pout-eyed, rouged at the disco we met,
Stone's alive, rock's afloat and yet...

Oh lovely braced in a silver candle,
Lift up your pink furlined toes
And slipper swim to me...

Bereavement and the soft ashes of dust
Brilliant-edged in the reckless toad air,
How I used to care...and now...I cannot
Any longer care...

Adrift, away and afloat
Pebbles on water...once I had a daughter.
Now I am too young...
Fine and fairly Joan,
Believe, believe, alone
And burningly, burningly concerned...

Worried, thirsty, hungry and afraid
A tiny smell of sympathy that strays
And mumbles baffled...

Marriage, marriage bloomed in white purples
Doomed with the flowers of the lilac tree
Dead to you is dead to me,
Is dead,

I'll take the flowers to your grave,
I'll spread the leaves and make them grave,
I'll...grave...and I'll steal,

Sitting on a shelf, beside a fire,
You are a bloody liar...you always were,

Oh God, days days of grey
And a year and now, limp with scars,
Beaten, hurt, beside the fire
Love paces, love paces
And stares
With a dove in her hair
And wrinkled mad hands,

Why is it seen like stone, like stone
That we are all, alone, alone?

What will you do to me when you love,
I'll buy for you a tiny dove,
I'll swing the world,
I'll wing and unfurl
My wings over you
    Until yours
    Are mine
And you cannot fly...

Love that lingers, love that drops,
Love among the apricots,
Far and yielding, close, ungreeting,
Come to me, love, oh sweeting, sweeting...

The years are old and grey now
In my hands, they melt my life with silence,
Shrinking bands of tattered beauties
Decorate the room with quiet
Doom, doom.

Oh, ancient, ancient and hurt and dead,
But I heard what you said
Before you were dead,
And I'll know what you said
Before you were dead
And when we're both dead
We'll know what we said.

THE ROSE   ▽

Love, pouring in flowers,
Bites with a bee
And stings in a sulky rose —
How could I leave thee, lovely frost-stung petals?
Your light that grows and glows and grows
Within, beside, around me, all, and
Around all those
Who love the sting and not the scent of roses.

Black willows draped with flags shine over the hasty momentous sea
That dipped in sunshine, soft as rice-shone turtles
Clambering with heavy neck and empty rocks
Out of the water to shake in the clear cypress
A thousand whirring dials of water. Flattered
And great, the willows lie, huge hulks
Stretched out in timorous harps that reach and pluck
The sea-blue whistle from a fading dying sky.

FINALE ▽

All my life I have struggled from gentleness
And men. Shaking off heatsteam
From the far, dry corners of desire. Kissing only
Where, in wet smooth black alleyways, the crows
Pack hunting in crowds.
And here, at the end of the tape, I feel sun
Beating on my shoulders like a light
And warm. To trust and kiss and love you
In clasping beauty. Teach me of
Wonderful silences, far in the glowing
Of your eyes, my tears.
Let my passion kill me.

As far and flat as a brushed-off grave
Under the white cocked hat of sky, swirl
Blue ribbons merrily and the land
Is striped and bare-loaded peasants; tired-backed
And warm the sun shoulders heavily up
The daisy-strangled hill and lies, in sweating gladness,
Pouring on the top. A twirp of sparrows
Clutchers and vicious noisily—autumn lakes
Are blue and clearly soft as lovers' dives
In evening. A grating wood and piled and broken axe
Sprawls yellow in the corn and sways, with a crooked
Tooth-edged smile. Life streaks down
In velvet bloomers and all is silent.

Hayfevered grins under red-black and red-blue-black
Coats that stream the land and dry the flowers
Into wine-stung, fly-eaten windmills, spinning pale and passionate,
High and gracefully between the wind's curved hands,
Belting through the air and flipping tops of trees
Like green coins to the ground—Autumn quivering comes
In a shirt as Summer's bikini droops and breasts
Wild as flowers tremble on the ground that laughs
And lashing laughs against her faint brown touch,
Weeds, bright as primroses, hail you, king of
Thorn and ancient, sitting, mushrooms on a bright wet step.

Flowers rough with the sandstone edge
Of cheek-chinked light, raft in the mists
And flake, tumble down
Into fires, until. . .I feel

    The strumming brum of a faint, free Mardi Gras
    Calling Paradiso in the west,
    Oh come, I come, waves flying
    Scarf aloft with transparent pleasure,
    I come to take an easy simple silent leisure
    At Mardi Gras with you.

Let me lay this burden down
Upon you, the sea whispers
Pale and pink,
Naked in dawn we pull
On our quiet dripping clothes
Watched by a gull,

    Skies worship,
    Loneliness in summer,
    Mardi Gras
    Who are you?

The child is crying,
The hotel is locked,
It was built, all right,
But the doors were often blocked by sand and silt
Drifted in by lovers,
However we don't care for such things,
After the Costa del Sol,
We found it almost droll.

    Light violins, light breezes, pale skies,
    Fresh lies in Summer's
    Dewy greens and thorn breaths,
    Silent dying laughter
    Whispers of births not deaths.

Mardi, oh Mardi, Tuesday Gras
And foie gras, really George
You shouldn't speak to a waiter like that,
They have feelings too. Oh really.
I do wish you'd take off that silly hat.

    Silver dawns, growths in the west
    Of tumbling bashful crystal waves
    Grinning in frantic mermaid sense
    That wailing, howling, yet engraves
    A silent monologue on the side of our ship,

Oh John, but sailing makes me sick,
I told you...

Did you ever get that far,
We did, but...

Oh silent, singing, singing Mardi Gras.

CAUSERIE ▽

Your sky is all trussed and lovely tonight
With its clearness and rose and sad sea-lined tears,
I feel as you steal, the lemon's sweet peel
Is falling and touching me deep with its fears,

Your hand slips in vain on the breast that is soaking
And wrapped in fresh milk and tied in fresh sacks
And eaten in pain and dissolved in the rain, leaving me
Who is vain to deceive those who lack.

My heart is a palace abandoned and lovely —
Beaten, I lie there, I die there, I sigh
And I find as I stroke the fine hair above me
I long for the fine hair that dots out your eyes.

My beauty, harsh-whipped in your soul, I have seen it
In your eyes of fire, in the eyes of a fair
Always playing, each day, and I know I must say
To you, darling, keep rag-wrapped from every beast's lair.

To me, fair love, you never shall be dead
Nor, living, fall in dreary shower,
For burning life which dresses all your head
In golden leaves caught from a dusty bower
And stolen, never weeps and creeps away
And all of Summer's candles are not burned
Alone and joyous in a single day
Where Beauty, loveless, sits and sunny learns
Of flowers and stars and seas and children's song
And lovers' feasts and midnight games and smiles.
Then will she gleesome rise and trot along
Lonely to cupboards? No, she keeps her wiles
    And leaves but, hiding, drops a sunshine tear
    Through which she glides and quickly reappears.

I caught a wind, love,
Held it like a horse,
Breaking violently, neighing, crying,
I held it tight, it choked,
I felt it was dying,
But, love, it's true
I was holding it for you, just you, my love.

I caught a flower, last night, love,
Breaking in the wind, it coloured tansy
And torn, a new bud, quick born,
From where you led me, quickly dead.

I caught the sky, I held the world,
I trapped the night and left it crying,
Crying with naked pity,
Fresh water smell and the early lilt of morning flowers
Helps me tell, oh darling,
How they and we were dying.

Flights of bluebirds carry the clouds
In empty swirling heads, and water rises
With the white and pearly sands to smile
And gorge on a drowning face. A frame of weeds
Sinks loose and brittle to the dark-edged bottom,
Trimming and flower-edged, fantastic snobberies
Waiting on the ground, around a smooth and
Silken skull, that golden waits and sits
And sands in beading eyes, that hollow wink
And catch a hollow wind who whistling waits
And peers in boring eyes through the broken fence.
A child is playing, soft-skinned and warm,
And tossing like the moon who bathes
Flat-backed on the lazy, smooth-skinned sea,
She laughs and falls like a white stag
Foaming to the ground and sinks
In empty clusters and twisting bubbles
Piping to the air and on the ground
A sea of vasts and empty lovely bodies.

Gay and bright in skinhead yellow the flowers kick
Hobnailed rooted in the silent skirts of earth,
I see Summer's sad smile dwindle to a wick
Of a candle barely burning before a birth,
I see you, lovely, fighting amongst the trees
For breath and feeling fragile as the seed
That made you, white-pearled, the seas
Live crazy and angry beside us, their need
Is older and greater than ours, your life
Is taller than mine, so push and make my smile
Gentle tell the harshness bitter and rife
In hatred against you, swallows over each mile
    Guilty and upset, beside your face,
    I see in your arrogance, mine and my disgrace.

Sweet essences move not the music sadly,
Nor I, nor you, my love, can pluck this tune
In sad expressionless tear, we see that gladly
The trees are shadowing close and sinking soon
And Summer on a lonely donkey rides
Through the silent sky, her eyes all washed
With tears of silent blue that bitter sides,
Her beauty's cheek to paling pulse is lost,
Oh love, cry out how all the flowers' garden
Bend their heads and sink in sadder thoughts of Spring
Long-buried, decked in glittering pardons
And on its knees by Autumn's glittering ring
    And knives that sharply cut the tortured sky
    And slash our loves together, you and I.

HARVEST FESTIVAL ▽

This is a poem written to be performed by six voices as well as a poem to be read. It was initially inspired by an episode in the film *Scum* where a 14-year-old red-headed Borstal boy is raped and commits suicide. The two 'She' voices should overlap and speak at speed. 'The Dance of the Vegetables' is to be read in a rapidly bouncing schoolmistress fashion (as in the style of the late Joyce Grenfell), 'Hallowe'en' in an unbroken, uncomprehending boy's voice, 'Into the Garden' by a madwoman, and 'Beside the Tomb' in blank-verse narrative. The whole poem is to be performed at top speed and without interruption.

Part One. The Dance of the Vegetables

She: Once I knew...
She: How in a silky garden lay...
Gurgle. Giggle. Splat. Plug. Stop.

A red sun in gardens sits crouched like a tree,
Hugely harnessed in shadows as pale as the sea,
Branching scarlet with dampness, it weeps and it blinks
And it wrings its pink arms as it helplessly sinks
And stumbling, lies trapped as Night springs from the ground
As the vegetables wake and start twitching around

With grumblings and achings and shakings of roots
Till the dark air is flying with dirt from their boots.
And resounding with swearing and quarrelling sounds
As the larger potatoes push carrots around,
As marrow fights marrow, tomatoes are killed
Slipping down in the riots on onion tears spilled.
Till, at last, with a blast, like the cry of the leek
As, lonely, through forests it wanders to seek
Its lover, the beetroot starts blaring his horn
And, purpling with sweat, he explains there's been born
A red-headed cauliflower, tiny and white,
Who tore himself free from his last roots, last night
And lies now, in silence, and gasping for air
On the freshest of topsoil, alone, over there.
The vegetables quivered with silence, but smiled
And padded like frogs down to see the new child,
They quietly squat for the chief beetroot's Grace,
That calls blessings upon the new cauliflower face.
The blessings soon over, they pray in a trance
Till the chief beetroot's second proposes the dance.
Then skipping round flatly in balances false
Forming strange, broken rings, they get ready to waltz.
And red partners green, as they're starting to spin
And even the weeds are allowed to join in.
Limping and straggling, their long yellow hair
Flies in colourful nets, streaking through the damp air.
Always quicker and brighter, they warm all around
Until, tall and exhausted they fall to the ground.
And the lines of the dance become stately and few
As all of the vegetables tireder grew.
One long coloured line left, still span in a wheel,
Each dancer remembering what vegetables feel
When they first sniff raw earth and they first feel the sound
Of their old tribal dancing that's rocking the ground.
Stomping nearer the baby and, cooing, they stroked
His white knobbled head and his darkly green throat.
Their colours all merging in flat, heavy grace,
Concentration scowled large on each vegetable face.
As exhausted they dropped to start seeding with pain
From their heavy exertions, it started to rain
And the rain fell down deep and the rain fell down black

Till the silence grew wet as they all scurried back
Pushing down the grey earth with their straddling flat leap,
Pushing down into darkness and dryness and sleep
And all of the flowers shudder deep in the ground
As the rain, clapping loudly, walks paddling around.
But all else lay silent. Apart in its bed
On the surface and waiting, the cauliflower head
With its white bulging skull, lay calm, hopeless and hurt
And still faintly smiling alone in the dirt.
Silent he waited and like a stone set
On his own, on the surface, alone in the wet.
And the vegetables sleeping, thought of his red head
And thought of the morning and him, dry and dead.
And, shaking with lust, they thought of their next chance,
Their next cauliflower birth, the next vegetable dance.

Part Two. Hallowe'en

She: Thee fair and light of gardens, oh, I bore fruit...
She: Peaches, slimy with golden drops, that black the fingers...
She: Smiling. Poison apples grew and bruised and blessed and slept...
She: Like candles burning...
She: Through the pale Night...
She: In a waxen garden. Death...
She: Far within a year...

I, Ginger Marmalade, of fourteen years and a grave, bequeath my smoky lantern to the quick grey path that marches from a white sand road. Let the tree's smoke fade to the tightening road, downwards and downwards, into a fast yellow fog. Touch not the white cherries where maggots, cradled, sleep beneath fruit. Nor may you forget my apples and candles. Scent the dark with pearls of light, I may touch or treasure. And let the angels pray...

Where bats float like apples, let me remember. An A was an apple, a B was a bed and a bat. Sweet brown bites that pock like fleas through cooling air. Oh, trickle down the open stars and save me, wretched, unbelievable. Long golden worms of lanterns curve and sway in stretching circles. Near, an apple caught hanging with a yellow bite. Scrape up the stars and launch the roof to dreary sandy light.

Drunken or fourteen, lurching in the rain. Desire, swift-edged, lies curling between the lips and laughter. Lurching, oh boyoh, lurching. And crows, woven from the bloody holes of night.

A swinging rope of lanterns. Yellow faces, beneath the grins, are blueish and water tight. Bright as fruit-juice in a fire. A lantern with a grinning stupid face. His yellow face...his yell...oh God...his yellow face.

She: And suddenly...
She: I saw him swinging, like a wire from a broken pole, and
/calling...
She: With birds crawling like flies on the autumn ground...
She: Heavily. Brown and heavy. Looking...
She: Stuffed with life...
She: Crazy without movement...
She: Picking out his eyes...
She: In madness without death...

Part Three. Into the Garden

Yes, by this fountain, white with stars,
I for my lover shall wait
And dream I see him, quick with tears,
Come rushing to me, late

And weeping. Weeping—the tears strong
Are flowering from his blue eyes
In soft red shadows, bright and long
And falling in glittering sighs.

'My love, my life, oh, tell me quick
Your grief, my darling sweet!'
'Oh trembling day, let down the sun
But do not lie in the heat.'

He answered, crying, trying to touch
The fingers of my hand,
His own cold fingers fall straight through
In brief, forgetting sand.

'My baby's tired,' he mutters low,
'My baby's gone to bed,
He's gone to play in slower dreams,
Our warmest bright is dead.'

His mottled face brakes screaming round
And, swollen, red and fine,
His glittering eyes march slowly out
And lay their look in mine.

'His wet plump body's yellow-cold,
His face is soft and bare,
I kiss his naked lips and stroke
His fine and bloodlit hair.

'I raise him high, I hold him low,
I push him at my breast,
I listen to his quiet heart
Unbeating in his chest.

'I lie him down in cushions green,
I comfort his cold hurt,
I kiss his hand, I love his face,
I cover him with dirt.'

My lover's smile all smooth and white
And wet, grows mad and grey,
I touch his voice, I feel his feet,
I feel him move away

And I sit, weeping, dark and black,
The fountain all alight,
I hear the water, flying fast
But quickly stained with night.

Too long I wait, until I wake
And know my dream's unsaid
Untrue. Thank God! I have no child
And none of mine is dead.

Too long I wait, oh God, too long
Unmoving I remain,
Beside this fountain's hanging light
My lover never came.

She: In the bitter end I shall die and be reborn as a tree...
She: Laden with flowers, kicking...
She: Under a purple sky...
She: Against Night and wild...
She: The violet, draped above the cold...
She: Round the coffin...
She: Damp earth...

Part Four. Beside the Tomb

Empty, dragging between a torn and threaded sea,
Sank barrels of weakened flowers, like pulses
Under the white rash of a braless moon
Beating beside a black island, and bent.
Stringing tunefully to hell,
And crooning in silent prayers for the dead.
The rings and stains of flying truth
Collapse in candles, apples in the darkness
Swell and tempt, calling in subdued clouds of sinking
Light. Oh, flight of life, defend me as a boy,
And small, against the night. The lantern's pale and knowing smile.
The ragged breath of candles.
Net me the bones that float upon the sea...

A was an apple, B was a bed, C shone a candle and D...is dead...
Perishing like feathers in a garden
Of broken weeds and compost, vegetables dancing,
I see a light, beside the piles of apples, piles of lanterns,
Fattening on a black island, I see
Where candle creeps between water and light,
The rich fruit, where bones feed, where bones lie,
Where bones lie in the water, on the sea
Floating in dreary white perfection.

She: Was it not, it was not, bones they said?
She: Bones, they said. Yes. Bones.

As words decay and lives decay as Summer falls
In ragged stripping bough, replaced by gold-
Crocked Autumn who foggy miser calls
To the fresh-bearded lambs, crying in the cold,
The world clasps its freezing hands together
Swinging in the fatal round
Of mortal joys and ugly treacherous weather
Flying hooded beyond an elliptical bound
Of fairness, fruits that wrinkled on the trees
Restore the blossom to the fruitful worms
Who greedy-stomached bruise the grassy lees
In sliding shades and evil fateful turn,
  And as the Summer's bruises turn blue and riper
  Autumn tints turn gold and play the piper.

White dripping autumn curls like dusky foxes
Behind a tawny coughing fire. Trees, once green and shelter-cupped
As springing, fresh-bud peas, open and flake their empty hands
In hissing fingers at the grating sky—black and empty,
Stark-switched and tree-lined, far away, walks Love
Misty and mumbling on weeding, half-torn paths,
Thorns on her face and hair and the smiling cloud
Bird-nestling in summer, falling, waits and weeps
Around her bare and thorn-speckled torn and gentle loving feet.

When seas in glittering sadness are greatly born
And vanquished, twinkling to a single star,
And virtue's rose plucks fairer from its thorn
And all things fairer show than fairer are,
The desert shaves his lonely head with sands
Of faint eternity, transparent love
In ribbons walks the isolated lands
And clouds shun dirt-edged skies that fill above
With ugly weeds and frightened flower-pitched sounds
All decorate with knee-dropped bowing feather
Plucked from a bowing bird whose sound resounds
Destroying heavenly music's flights together,
  And all things die and all things mortalise
  And look through powdered glass with weary eyes.

The sun swells bare and blocked on the glittered leaves
Cold at sunrise and shivering by ancient corn
Cascading true and yellow, it faintly bereaves
With speechless anguish the darkness of the dawn
But when the sun, like a dark-edged blister set
On the nape of the world, frowns and glaring lies
With burning head above the streaking wet
That bristles beneath its single staring eyes,
I see the forest walk wet through the rose
And cuddling trap its finer speed away
Until in swelling groves it solemnly goes
And hangs in ghastly green in glimmering day,
  And all the sun in heavenly show grows darker
  Beneath the night's diseased hand paling sharper.

Dark and lying in lustres through the pink remains of light
Crows emptiness like a carcase, broken with whirring flies
And hard in cracked-out bones. The sun is bleached
And rises, scarlet-raw to pink in scattered scabs
On white clean-laden sky. Death moves within,
Me longing for its sharp black bite and teeth as
Oyster-buried and cool as the rocking beds of coal.
Ah hell, claim me here, chained and silverstruck
Slave to your desire, and write in letters on my face,
Here lies one broken, bitter, banished and disgraced.

Dancing light as bluebells colours the earth
In sad and strumming melodies, come the winter storms
And come the blooms of spring, I cannot count the time
Racing in vivid harebells bright and past
Beyond the winter blast that tugs in teeth
Beyond the golden autumn's last.

Flat and smuggling on the ground
In yellow flights of tunnels, swings the light
And harmless falls in golden alcoholic stupor
Through a lazy afternoon. Oh whiteness, corrupt
And lepered, chewing the air in sickness
And contempts of a brightness, once revealed
And never found but in the bulging thick red skins
Of scorched tomatoes, burst and bleeding on the earth
In bloody boneless skulls. The green and piercing nails
Of trees scratch the white and scabbing sky,
Weather hangs heavy like a horse,
And rides in clouds and moons. The sea
Is pushing like a child against a boat
And twits and bubbles like a raft in stinking cream,
Sinking lives and twists of outward feelings
Curl in the eyes of a penguin, cold and hard
And gazing in mad black-whiteness out to sea.

And willows bend and grace single over a lonely waterfall,
Weeds, hanging like crowns, dip purple into the empty sways of water
And rustling, winkle, sleep and droop
In horning fingers, calling over the moors in a mist
And slender as abandoned straggles of wind in the rain.

▽

Look in your glass and speak to me of death
And sweet mortality, running like a stag
Wild and white outside of love's vague breath
That tattered wipes its mirror with ugly rag,
See fields without you, trees that empty bare
Are joyful in their naked certain truth
And Winter's lovely hands around her empty stare
That faintly talks of frost and hints aloof
Of madness, nothing, man the rabbit born
Who stands like a sheep and walks with nerveless ease
Under the night and under the stars of dawn
In careless raptures, fades between the trees
    Below the earth, with wilful lazy stare,
    Who careless shows with lovely naked care.

▽

Sad deserted shore, fickle as a waste
That brands in dirty purple, launched above the sea
And crying desolate for the lovely milks of earth
To scatter abandoned and careless down upon,
Its shaven stubble frost.

As petal clocks wash down in dusky red
And watery weep their old tears by the gates
That wicked wobble limping as they bled
On ancient hinges bent and slow and late
To open, I think your face is silver clear
And young in startled loveliness that glows
Where dry-eyed Time sits wailing by the bier
And scattering purple poppies where she goes,
And with these seamless passions in your features
You shame the trees to drop their yellow leaves
And black and lovely naked stand your teachers
Of shameless Time who lusts between the eaves,
    And in white dated body you cast your vote
    To reveal the time in slender killing note.

Wild lonely guitars rocking in a silver-starred night,
Falling, lonely, flying in a nervous sound,
Birds cooing like hornets. A breeze scratches itself
Under a feeble, sitting rock, dropped for a rest
And stuck. Nature sprawls
Hard and knitting under a hundred-foot oak,
Bored she lights a fag for herself and starts to smoke,
Causing a lover, walking, hands linked in his own
And kissing himself feverishly, to mention casual,
It's time to be getting home, to be warm,
And a hopeful liar, to suggest the way
Lies through the trees and on the bed near
This sudden bonfire.

When shuddering leaves are yellowed in the cold
And grin with age and smooth like parchment skull,
And twisted birds, like half-skinned ladies, bold
Chirp out their bony chants that fall in lulls,
And in the brighter orange autumn air
Tinted in frost, I see the lines that trace
In withered turnings all of Winter's stare
That glints out hollow from her colder face,
The tossing fire that drapes in orange scarves
Around the houses lights her in its folds
And shows her bleak and beauteous, black in halves
Of sultry shadow, pale ice in the cold's
    Busy fingers twisting through the frost
    Proclaiming her kingdom, proclaiming we are lost.

MOON   ▽

This blue-rinse moon who peers old and weary
Through the cracks of scudding earth—flaming craters
And hazy plains lie taut and straight and blind
In white to her. Your wrinkled yellow smiles
Droop tired on our faces bright and spring as flowers
And light us rancid pale, we glow like worms
In love for you, old faded sweetness
Who still, one crutched arm dropped,
Spreads scattered light, thick and warm
As a stream of shimmering cloud
Through the empty dark and piercing it
A needle of broken snow.

CASSANDRA

I

Black, black and deep gold settles Night
Like a star-touched crow; a little dust
In faint, dark scraps begins to creep
And spin between the sleeping roofs, it drops
Onto the dancing grass, and crackling
Water, within a nestling wind that falls
In soft black feathers down to earth. Sharply
A church clock calls out amongst the huts,
Cassandra strikes and, with a scream, is born.
Inside the smallest hut, wind-eaten,
A candle sucks in coarse night air and breathes
Back smooth-skinned light, the mother whines and
Breaks to greet her child, who, kicking, bloody
On a green baize mat, punches the air, chokes,
And tries to smile. Curtains, soft and white,
Of baby's love fall cooing to the ground.
Cassandra, wilful, kicks, screams and kicks
Again. The mother moans until her child is rocked
And hushed, while, outside, listening
Sits the wind, pricked up, and stark mad he
Lifts his feet and pushes broken leaves
At empty branches, annoys the sky
Who waits with a quiet frown, for the child
To sleep. She yawns and all is silent.
Broken dreams walk sobbing together
Along the even breaths of calmer breeze.
And Night waits singing quiet as a swan
For Dawn. She flounces to pull pink curtains
Miles apart and, smiling her reddened teeth,
She wipes the sticky sun that lies in long
Thin streaks of golden grease, amongst harsh cloud.
Embarrassed by the light, the grasses slow
And cease and leave their hopeful nightly dance.
Plank rests on plank, silent walls sleep
In the motionless ground. Dust rises
From the green sun-topped wood and spreads
In crawling moss along the thickened light

To gather round a broken window-pane
Where the baby points.

II

Rainbow-tossed seasons float and fall in
Dark heaps of years. Cassandra grows and
Watching the night-times chasing light, she learns how
The sun will drain to water when she's caught.
Slipping sweetly up the fairy-tale
Ladder, she became more beautiful
Than wise. In strange, bright fashion, helpless
As a star, she rushed through time with grace,
Pushing aside all bitter branches of experience
And passing beyond. For eighteen years
Between a soul and stars, she crawled,
Like a nervous bird, onto the tip
Of settling dark. There, she waits nightly,
Strewn across the broken window pane,
A white and scattered mess of sparks, until,
One night a blinking drunk stumbled beneath her hut,
While she, in whiteness, steadily shone above,
Like a child, with large unfeeling eyes
That gaped at his swaying picture. He,
Half-awake and disbelieving, peered
Then flung a shaking stone to break the
Ripples of her presence, but his hand
Stuck in hazy fume, and pulled back the air,
Letting the stone drop harmless down. She,
Seeing his intent, and furious, comes
Rushing down to scold and to slap him.
Eager he listens for the running steps
That sweep along decrepit stairs and slip,
And, trembling, land in whiteness, at his
Waiting feet. He, quickening, his brown gold head
Suddenly smeared in shadow, bends to
Raise her and falls himself instead and
Dizzy swims between her pale arms and legs.
Trying to kiss, he tore her hair and scratched
Her struggling face. He wrenches at her clothes,
Clawing, tearing and biting the startled
White and rapes her with lingering love.

Through it all, her tears ran fast and silent
As a wasting stream, till his final blow
That left her still, while he, panting, growling,
Ran, frantic in colourful elation,
Away. She lay, quiet as a child
In sweetest rest, and wept and slept and woke
Finally, when day ran puffing up
The slopes and shot the sun like a tarnished
Bullet at the blurred air. Then she rose,
Deep in murderous dreams of pregnancy,
And looked at the sun and laughed aloud.
She ran to gather daisies, sweet for
Throwing and threading between the clouds
To trip up Night, and felt the air come,
Purple-dyed and filleted, diving round
In hops that picked her body full of
Slanders. She dashes off to kill her mad
And frightened tracks in water, stamps on stones
Her mind in flames, her hair loosens in
Greasy cords that pull, flying in a net
Around her face. She paddles, stamps and moans
To see water flake away in diamonds
From her cold feet. Fainting, and unclean,
Cassandra wanders in tears back home.
Where, wild-eyed but patient still, she seeks
Her mother for the final time. Her mother,
Frightened, listens and demands her reason.
Cassandra will not say, but runs from
The hut like a colt, stealing white grapes
And dripping milk that she crams in her
Frightened mouth like cream, trying to cleanse
Her aching mind.

III

Trailing dirt and fieldmice, like a goddess,
She stalked the bleak, bare fields and lived
Off stalks and tiny animals she killed
As they rushed for comfort into her gentle hands.
Beast followed beast, hot grey squirrels,
Voles and creeping owls, distrustful starlings,

Silent sheep who listened without reply,
Came to hear the rings and stains of truth,
She muttered, in half brief tears, mad as
Sunshine. Greater beasts followed, men who
Heard the name 'Cassandra' like a wind
Cool through their minds. Women, silent at
Her fate, pulled children in her vague
And straying path, to catch her word of
Favour or of fear. Waited for the wide
Unfrightened lips to betray bright promises.
So Cassandra swayed along her road
Pursued by tearful children, faltering
Adults and animals, hopping after
Eager to bite. Each day, the crowd increased,
Each day it nobler grew, and sharper
At needling in her words and pinning truths,
Until, under a fair and honest sun,
The King arrived. The papers were informed,
Cameras sprung out the earth like nervous
Rabbits, cast in steel, to watch. The King
Was wary; in his eyes, Hope danced like
A goat on a grave. He moved to
Cassandra, in flailing majesty.
She cast her eyes down, murmuring to herself
Fanciful jangles of sky and stars,
Of golden deaths, of all deaths, save of one
That strolled in lonely life, praying with prayer
Ungranted. Seeing her now, in ragged
Stripping beauty, he, curious, raised
His hand to touch her hair but she, she
Moved aside and staring from large pale eyes
Demanded what he could want with her.
Between mother and rape, this, the first time
She had spoken direct. It silenced the crowd
Who scurried aside like ants on a
Sunny branch, eager to gorge on light,
Uneager to be trapped. She asks again
And he, blushing, saw his Royalty
Withered and dead at her feet. He coughed
And in a hard dry voice, begged her for
His greatness. He was a King, he said,

Who'd tended mounds of people to blossoming
Happiness, helped grow trees and ships, and
Had planted in his Palace the questions
Of the poor. Cultivating Art, he'd
Introduced a Christ and set him high
On sharp rocks, preaching tolerance. He'd
Washed his face in blind humility
All his life, brought joy to all, but, yet
Had found a dark wart, like a sore
That scratched his mind and bled on all his thoughts.
Thus, distressed, he knew he was not King
Until he'd conquered this within himself.
What could she tell about his golden country,
His lovely Dorado to lift it up
Whole to a pile of flaming life? She turned
With quiet eyes in his and whispered,
Whispered in a low, dead voice, her gaze on
His brown head, of midnight, dooms and deaths.
Of despairs sweeter than light, of livid
Fires around his golden land, his mind.
Of truth, the small black hole that splits
Like a wart, and breaks in a basin
Of sticking black and tears away again
Into a dirty abyss, halving
The world and wrenching space
Into a silent, bitterdark atom
Single and free. This, she whispered, was the
Answer, was the cancerous wart that ate
His life, casting briefly wilful shadows
Of worth around his mind. Go with the crow,
Cassandra muttered, who's clinging to your
Back with bloody claws, and kill, let the
Country tumble down. Silent, she hurled
Her wild eyes to the ground and stepped away.
He lifts his curly head and feels darkness
Moving above and silence beneath. He
Gropes at the pale girl, shocked, and blinking
Sees her, flimsy and fresh as a water
Lily. Clumsy he pulls out a fist and
Strikes her on the cheek, moving away
As, with a cry, she falls. Quick blood runs

Out like water into the bending grass.
The King leaves and the crowd swarm off like ants
Who've smelled fresh meat. The girl waits in the field
Blind until the sun dies and Night with early
Dragging tread limps in. A different Night
In different form, both clear and white
And shining through the planet like bright glass.
Through the sharp crystal, round Cassandra's feet
Grow soft brown ruffles, flames begin to turn
And grub in tiny orange leaps that reach her knees
And, growing, thickening in the white air,
They caught her waist and stretched in vivid
Belts and tongues. Slowly she rose and brought
Large flames, while small ones ran behind
In tiny swirls, tracing a brown and bitter path.
Shooting beyond to her shoulders, the orange curled
And whispered in her ear. Slowly she lifts her arm
Pressing it against the white clear Night
Towering in glass all around. She knows now
In colours, vivid and translucent,
The haughtiness of life, reds and purples
Swinging beneath a heavy lace-white net.
Caught to the eyes in flames, she walks the clean
Air, her hair, heavy with brilliant
Splinters, flaming behind. Graceful, Cassandra
Strides from the empty fields into a silence
Of blackness and forests, huge firs, bending
And dark from the night cover her. She fades unseen
And unknown, except by some, the mad and miserable.
They sing of sweet Cassandra, now a battered crone,
Who, wandering in the dark, forever sniffs
At broken roses, wrenches rags and webs
And lets the sky, greying and huge, perch
On her shoulder, while the wind, at her feet
Nuzzles the old and half-forgotten flames.

Ulysses lay tied and beachbound, his foot held by a stake
And the rear of his arms sunburned and broken by
The vivid staring sky, that fell in April, as he tried
To make an escape from the isles of men who,
Lined in dusty lanes, crowded and teeth shown,
Barked at him—we all saw his pale face
Frightened in the moon's dim liquid glow
And silent earth-spinning chants of early sacrifice
On a harvest's song that sprang like dead machines
Red and hard in the April snow.
Ulysses, agonied, bare and boned, alone
He sleeps and digs his grave alone
And flowers have no place for him,
All of life is dead and hardening rapidly
In the sure-fire glance that springs in thudding coals
For his coal-blown head. Empty Ulysses rock
And in your toil, leave us the buckets that briefly
Boil in Hell's sweet silent paths.
Leave us your soul.

Darling come...one...two...dance...one...two...glance...

Angel feathers, hairy beast,
Keep from me the Night's pale feast;
Little child and white am I
Innocent as April sky;
Come my love and keep from me
The Devil's cares and sleep with me,

Black blossoms white on a snowy tree branch. I see the world rise and
pull swelling away from her sister sun—I mould the earth, I mould seas,
glittering seas, stringing them up with delicate foam, each sweet strangler
gleams an hour and goes. Oh I, oh I am delicate as pearls—fetch me a
mirror, show me my loveliness. Fading and pulsing like a child's star held
and clasped at midnight.

My love I'll take you at midnight,
My love I'll come at midnight,
My love the green and gold,
My love, my stars and soul,

Biblical cant
Preaching rant
A see and a saw
And a Minotaur...

As I walked up from Thebes one day
A hornèd beast stood in my way,
With a great long beard and a swishing tail
So I pushed him down and set my sail,

And I ran off quickly from that shore
And I looked back once to the great seashore
And I found it was the Minotaur
That I kicked and knocked, what else did I find?
Oh my love, that my Minotaur was blind.

Just this way...one...two...three steps left. Oh the sky is chill tonight
with the evening's fading purple wings...we can ride it like
horses...braying...braying...neighing...lift up your wings and
fly...

Ivory eyes, I see them closing white as silk,
And long-legged, lashed, clammy and milky
I'm led with my wings, aflapp on the ground,
And the stars sound;
The stars sound,
Oh Christ rocked in a bosom mild
They lead me with a little child;
Gentle Jesus, sweet and kind,
Why am I blind?

Ulysses works with monstrous toil
To carry the world, to steal your soul;
Ulysses comes and carries away
The souls of the world to Hell, he says.

Seven days to make out light from the vivid dark, to find a glass in
which, when all things come to pass, I could find myself and lurk in
glittering dewdrop tears around myself and myself and blind...and
blind...

Far away rock away, love, he said,
Lead me here and I'll soon be dead,
And the cliff fell dark and it tumbled sharp
to the lonely houses, where only the lark
Sits brooding on a branch and scratches fleas
That creep between her wings and crawl up her knees.

Oh gentle Jesus, meek and mild,
Take pity on a little child,
Oh gentle child who's blonde and four
Take pity on a Minotaur,

Sky rocks, earth rocks, stars rock.
Rock. Rock. Rock.
Laughter in glen.
Why won't you come then and play?
Oh, only four, don't shut the door,
It won't be so hot another day,
Oh only four don't shut the door.
And the trees are winking in the shade,
Oh only four...
I'm going off to play, darling Minotaur,
But you stay still, I'll be back one day,

Oh only four and a Minotaur
Oh only mind and blind.

Ulysses, Ulysses on the beach and lying,
Throw at him stones and tie him, tie him,

Only four and a Minotaur

Bind him, bind him, sweet and bright,
And leave him cold in the egg of night.

Signed and blinded.

Let him catch...catch...catch...

He's long, he's dead, he's lined...and a corpse...he's dead...and a corpse...and a...lined...wrinkled...what corpse...blind...

Bray. Bray. Let the Horses neigh,
Give them fresh pasture at the end of the day,
When the Night comes and the noise is too loud
We'll all stab them hard and hang them in a shroud.

The sun hangs like a red ball over the sea at night, in wistful cotton...

The shells at the bottom of the sea are rotten...

Which way now...one...two...oh, you're tripping...
'Bye, my lovely Minotaur,
It's time to play, I'm only four,
'Bye my lovely Minotaur,
It's bedtime now, I'll shut the door
And climb in bed and there I'll see
You braying through the door at me,
But Minotaur, I'm only four
But big enough to slam the door.

When I consider life and all it grows
Seeks busily the circus that it makes
And fine trapezes, glittering its shows
With famous lines and faces, lovely fakes
Like Summer, the lonely freak, who fades
Into tipped blackcurrants brushing stark
Against white blossom, fantastic blades
Hurled by the wildblade Autumn through her dark,
And all ringmastered by the pushy Time
Who, whip aloft, nose red, will start to sing
Old ballads pulsing with strange unbeaten rhyme
In pushing players back and forth from the ring,
    And audiences still with life who gaze
    In silent wonder at him all their days.

Dreams that lace their shuddering shadows transcend
All mortal beliefs, the grey winding road
That sparkles to a dewy turnstile by the end
Rocked by the wind and silent nudely showed;
Bitterness, wretched, clasping at a tree
For its mad and muddy flowers, crying sinks
In forlorn existence tracing a dim expiry
Between the pins of Art and Nature's links
Forged anew with craftsmanship; when you in startled bright
Roll up your sleeves and face fixed to water
Clear and dead, your hair is lovely light,
Your face in Time's grizzled mirror long grown shorter,
    I see, in life's reflections, all that seems
    Flash rolling back to lined and sullen dreams.

L'HOMME ET LA MER ▽

The silent waves unrolling like a lake
Before you silent, noticing your soul,
Relieved to find the wool that you awake,
Will leave you free to tremble with its teasing roll.

Sink deep and trace the mirror of your water
In your eyes, your lips, your sweet name of love
And savage tragic dreams of sunny daughters
Bowed by the waves and bred by the doves.

You are two shadows, each discreet,
Each violent, your ruin is your pride
And with the sea, your silent ever sweet,
You sweetly leave the jealousy you died.

And yet as Time runs out along the waves
And perches barefoot, I see your hateful glance
Beyond remorse, beyond the life it craves
And silent with its everflowing chance.

▽

Madonna of the silver-faced moon,
Look down gentle and close on this shy and bantered loneliness
Sprung from the dry roots of many forgotten roots
And flowering now in bitterness, cold and hard, the tubers
Of baked earth tear in strips of flattened coloured life
And breath with dampness of fresh-stained, mown-off leaves,
Madonna of silvers, lady of rosy grapefruits and passions
Drifting green and slow through fragrant tears of rain,
Bless the earth to fruit and raise life, high and bold
And blonde as freshest tinted sunlights.

Lady of life, to whom with weary sage
I make my plea and place my duty down,
Take from me here this busy whittling page
And darken its margins with your careful frown,
Margins alive which darkness pure as mine
Cannot regret, in wishing love to show it,
Unless I believe some greater laugh of thine
Will giddily fall and handsomely bestow it,
Till all these stars that flake me with their fire
Clap in their aisles on glittering altars set
And place my confidence in their lovely choir
That dresses the moon and paints the sky still yet,
    For then I will know how far I can realise this
    Which, safe in my arms, is only dark promise of bliss.

My glass lies to me often, in beauty's gaze
Of lovely forehead, decent eyes and nose
A little elongated, maybe dropped sideways
And pinkish like the smoulderings of a rose,
And why should I care? Had I the loveliest face
And you were here, your smile would be more sweet
Less often, mine would be the odd disgrace,
To fall from perfection, perfection being neatness
And harmony in all, and I, disharmoured show,
With my nose and wrinkles, all that you might yearn
To see, or all that makes you yearn to go
And pass your nights with single solitary burning
    Candles, fluttering soft in the night
    Far brighter than me, why should I claim to be bright?

Green and yellow dusky gold
Lilies through the silent dawn
Crying in sparkling tears above
Her lost lover, the sea—battered
And broken, white-faced against the rocks,
We missed you, lost girl, trapped in green foams
Forgotten, away from the winds
Sweeping the lazy shore with dust
And brittle dirts from a Paradise long lost,
Never seen, unrecognised by God and man —
A silver bucket swinging from the moon
And cloaked in stars, stands
And leaks its light over the white and ghost-strewn phantom beach.

Like the sea throbs its green-gained hand across
The mouth of the coarse-toothed shore, our faint lives
Flake high and fall together, each sad cold loss
In frightened breath that gapes in frightened dives
Beneath the sea's cold touch, and angry waves
That chopping-faced draw close and grumble plain
All vanish in the foam's untouched sweet graves
That glitter lightly dropping in the rain,
So vanished love as faint and free as dew
Falls out in sparkles, laughing in the sun,
And then droops back and down and dims in few
Faint twinkles in the heels that run,
    And love that swirling highly fades away
    May yet drown deep and lost in sunset day.

LA BEAUTÉ

Alas I am mortalised! Like dreams of stone
And breasts where, turning, turning, each dies,
All done for fear of lovely love
Destroyed by poets forever silently dumb.

I wait in the sky on thrones, misunderstood,
Misbelieved, my heart where snow rains like swans
Distorting in grace the love of my face
Where I never yet loved, nor yet hated.

You busy poets, stuck and signed before me,
From whom I steal all greatest hopes,
Will eat out and up your days in blind study.
While I, to tempt your fragile cares,
Will show you mirrors believing all things,
Will show you my eyes and their mirrors of life.

I love you like an island, lying deep and stretched in valleys
Of darkest corn that grows at night and peaks and rises
Each mournful sweet day—love grows, empty and amiable
As a weak-petalled flower, simply ageing and soft
As deserted nettles, broken and freshed by each sharp and unexpected
Pin of rain, dripping silver as milk from the cloudy breasts
That overshadow and empty and pull and drag juices
Heavy and distilled from torrents of tender earth;
Gold, hard as mud and heavy, shifts and sparkles
Beneath the metal dust and shoots up into peak-topped trees,
They sway in winds and fall melted like ice to the ground,
So yellow turns silver and leaks away
Like the coming of stars fresh-picked and peeled
From the lemon juice of bitter draining day.

△

Sweet Valentine, the one-eyed misty gold of flowers
In me falls drooping blocked in sunshine tear
As Love in her cocoon and late-asleep this year
Rocks out and warbles, chants in scented gold
From trembled yellow lacies. A buttery celandine
Walks, sprawls and kicks soft-cupped beneath the
Tender smiles of winds. I dip in light
To meet your dark and shadow hair and lilt
In glimmering flight from your eyes as they to me
Pass secret, shadow-hid in buried dark,
But hold in fright, with soft and flower-edged mark.

△

As seas with rocking croon the mountains' lift
And silver waves lift dripping with the fish
In palely-lit sands, caught with dim swords' sift
That smiles and drips all trembling with the swish
Of the silver night caught fishing in the dark
Alone and bright, fainting lovely as its arms
Grip lonely around you like the feather-tongued shark
That graceful swims and smiles beyond all harm,
Oh darling lonely swimming in the sea's great might
Hold out your arms to me and swing me, sweet,
Till the waves touch the sky and darkness tinges light
And all the earth and tides may rise and meet,
        And then, oh love, in the lonely ocean's blast
        We'll celebrate our love and worship all our past.

A final hopeless poem, dead with pain
And sticking with love to the page,
Within these simple, cross-checked lines
Of black and white, you'll find
If you know truth, your happiness
Chirping on every line.

Was ever young love so chillingly told
From the old to the young from the young to the old?
Compassion is grave when the bearer lies dead —
Was ever young love so chillingly said?

Smart as rosebuds dangling between trees
And smooth as tender white skulls
The grave-lit flowers are lovely tonight;
They seek me, I cease them, we give them flight.

As clocks break down and throw in thistleseed,
And frantic walking day steps high and proud
And glares at hideous Night who, in need
Of loveliness, slinks after whistling loud
And waving his black-gloved hand in sane despair
And violent hope that staggers as he walks
With abandoned love and silent reproachful stare
Behind the back of careless Summer's talk,
And trees that whistle naked in the dust
Flatter wicked the early Summer light
And, flattening fists that push down in their lust,
They stretch and gape after, tripping old blind Night
    Who tapping slowly with his soft white stick
    Notices the seasons' clock and their timely prick.

In the early evening's mourning, we hear
The rancid coughings of a faint blackbird,
Bleaking on thorned-out branches, crying Murder!
Murder! Oh God, Time and Death both draw near.

The swift-flying skirts of clouds
Loop and rise to the hasty summer swallows.
Life flies and out, cold-boned and bare
On the bleak brown rock, flowers die
And Autumn perils, tottering close
To blind and scarfaced Winter, naked callous theft
Rises screaming like wind to the skies,
Harsh loves perish like blue-bottles
Once plump and black and flying
Like whirring saws through the bust and bleeding air.

I saw a moon once, floating broad and pale on water,
That surrendered monthly her bloody milk
Deep to the lavish cares of wanton Nights. In sleep here
With me and a knife in my mouth—catch up
Rotten tides and breaking foams, far from the stinks
Of seaweed and dead seabirds and the foams
All far and white and floating in naked carelessness
Down the bays. I cared once for lives that slung
From clifftops and wretched in careless spite
High above the reckless desperate light.

Green and cunning winters lope sleepy in
Like running stags round a whirlpool —
The air is bristling with its bleak unshaven beard
And mutters, trembles at the quickening touch it hates
And, breeding, snitters like a lark—empty in dew-filled grass
And spoken, her swingings written in deadly silken plume
And trembling guns that point and shatter, fire
Leaving no explosion.

Lullay, lullay Kattrin is white
And feeble from dying in the star's pale black light.
Sing songs of wild death, as Kattrin saw some
Angels were sleeping by a silver drum.

Lullay, lullay these boots are swift red
And French and alone by the wagon that's dead,
Sausage and shirttail and rabbit and run
In the bright cry of bullets beneath the black sun.

Lullay oh lullay and Kattrin is white
And knitting for her husband all through the pale night,
Lullay oh lullay oh Kattrin is red
On the roof for a husband and bootless and dead.

As wasted days skip painful through the year
And old, I watch the tremblings of my hand
Grow light and greener with the cheer
That's like delirious Summer twisting bland
To gape at Winter's startled teeth, biting behind
In eager greedy crows, flash-winged and grown
To mammoth creatures, gorging on my mind,
That spread and huged from tiny nestlings sown,
And as they break the branches, winter seed
Grows cruel and bitter close, I see in fright
That Winter's red was dressed in Summer's weed
And strangles from the branches strewn in light,
    So carelessly I glanced behind and saw
    How Winter pulled and slammed on Summer's door.

A single swan's call—high, a lovely note
Breathing gold above the world's foul breath,
A shout of light and dazzling sudden vivid white
The legs falter and fall, the wings
Sink in sudden hurricane
Beneath a cloud and plunge,
The lonely dying bird proclaims the air.

ALCESTIS

Let the dust raise her and bear her
In the breath of the sweet-toothed stars
And angels wrap their heavenly smiles
Around her silken shining for warmth and breath,
For Death has come and holds his bitter arms high above her
And from his face comes smoke, his eyes pool in tears
Of dimlit blackness, mists over a tomb,
As the violet weeps, abandoned, lonely fragrance
Stealing like a nightlamp through Dawn's
White heavy wings, sodden with tears, hasty feathers
Drooping in spicy dampness onto the arch ground;
Alcestis, take a lover, and carry him with you
To kiss Death in that far and lonely place,
A loverless Hell, and make him kiss Death for you
And tighten the blushes on your sickening
Paling face in the golden blush of fresh life's sun and breath.

△

Let those in proud honour with stars
Confess and doom below the ocean's edge
Where the starfish pluck and dented in lovely bars
Blossoming rich against the seething sedge.
Flowers spreading against the simmering sky
Rose and compassionate, thorns that breed like snow,
Stealthily cream and, stretching into a sigh
Of fragrance restored, silent love blows,
And terrible soldiers, passing for bloom
As they lay their swords in scarlet silk
On the deadening green and whimpering, soon
Are found to be dead and running like milk
    Under the leaves around the poise
    Of the silent lilies quiet in noise.

Death's tinny rage clangs out and brighter beats
In darker swathes between the negroid flowers
That sunburned bruise in hellish tapping feet
That regular fight the silent tempting hours
Creeping along on frightened flatfoot stamp
Between the day's bright lamp-posts set in gaps
Of shining appointments; ruthless with her lamp
She summons shadowed Night to pitch her maps
In altitudes of halving light and shadow
Settling on weary peaks with quarrelling face
That linked in split black-whiteness all the glow
That galvanises every living place,
    And, from these versions, fall the lips of man
    Who speaks in light is silent when he can.

LARKS IN THE MORNING   ▽

Caught between snow and Spring
Two larks, watery and dew-fallen
Between their wings, sat on a tree
And sang until the sunlight gold between the leaves
Turned green and listened—each one quiet
Pecking against the sky, head high-tilted,
Beaks wide as breaking swelling crests,
Fell into glorious song and the sun
Ran puffing up to light and listened.
Each felt darkness stir within them in
Nightly subdued response and noticed shadow on the tree,
The flushing face of worried day drew
High and clear in shining tones above
And movement caught the shadows,
Drawing them closer into one—each bird
Sang tireless until glittering day drew up in her
Full and glorious height and, trembling,
They each looked and fell into the sun
And, frightened, flew away.

LARKS AT BREAKFAST

The bruising sun shoots its blue skybrow
And love restlessly flies out like a butter-flower;
Within its nip of gold, I find your voice
Falling and flashing in a faintly silver shower.

But how could you see? How, within this black,
Where I see only the trees' fingers are long and bare
And pulling creeply dark against the shaking broken air?
How could you, blind, see back?

The clowning, coloured fingers pulled and crawl against me
And, fiddling, pick the linen of my wing,
But touches of branches tight within my heart
Thorn it to sing.

And yet you flew? And yet you called in bliss?
To beat out dreary and soft beside the picking air
The trembling frames of music. What music was this?

My feathers are smooth and straight beside your claws;
My beak in curved and patterned rests lies close to yours.
The wind shall rise and rush between us both
In tangled scurries: I see it run
As we lie straight and bright within the sun.

Each quiet move
Breathes fright,
Each noiseless shift
Calls flight
And these touches of the light-fingered sun
Pull out night.

Creep, love, soft within this silver cage,
Lift your wing and hide,
I feel the beating dark behind the stars
Fall pouring around us as we creep aside.

I come, I come as light does trembling pull her shining face
Out from beneath Night's hand.

Pick out the softest nettle for our bed,
Lay your feathering cheek down on my stretched and open wings,
Let purity sweep large and white and fall
In twisting apple dreams against us, listen to her as she sings.

I hear, I hear the silvering flows of Night
Pull foaming back, then walk towards the still and naked sand.

Touch, sweetness, out the sadness deep in me and sailing softly
Over my peckish heart to yours, open out those far and pale-flung
/wings,
Oh, lay them great around me, that I may, trembling, know your
/tremble
And feel in fear your frightened start.

I touch, I touch, I feel the ground shift singing
And Night lies great above us; as I reach to touch your lightness
I touch her darkly winging.

The wild swans are flying mad in a mist tonight
And their eyes are ravished pale and their skin
Is skimmed with light
As they twirling fly
Across the moonlit rocky hagridden sky.

The swan that bowed in a dream to me
Was cool and white and bent sparkling with ice
Asking for a terrible price for his ride in the stars,
Beyond wind, beyond worlds, too wild for words,
All that we are is what we are.

Why do I see these swans, wild and broken
Phantoms riding the sky
Beyond the lying pale breaths of Winter,
Beyond the lives that cobweb themselves in early icy bitter deaths,
The swans ride again tonight
Wild and pale and high.

What wish will hurt these silent swans
Who mocking mirror round
The silent stars, their dead heartbeat
The silent river's sound?

Oh you who haunt with shadows pale
And glistening long and strained
Beyond your beaks, your silver tails,
I hear the footsteps of the rain,

I see the lilies on your face,
The dirt line on your wing
And watching you, I see the dew
Fall crystallising in a ring

Of long-lost lovers buried deep
And drowned as by your feathers
They clutched and rode the storm
And beat your wings about the weather.

The Universe is pale and strange
And huge to them as me
And travelling still, pale and deranged
I wait to come to the sea.

The wild swans I saw at Coole last year
Beat me like mermaids strewing the clouds
And devilled with lustful virgin cloaks
They beat my life with broken wings;
The wind cries out, a lily sings
And through it all the dead sea chokes.

Rose-blossom fools the wisest amongst us
By the beauty of its smell
And the sweet lift of a swan's wing
Cowers beneath it as well.

Why swans, why me and the swans and you?
I have known eternities, lifted to the stars
Still beating and wingless, how I have loved
The purple flowers of life as she bends
And swings her gold chain, singing and linked
With fatal pale-petalled oars
Over the long ride to death. How could we know this?
I saw you as a bride, failing with orange blossom,
Apple-cherries in the burning dark
And beds of celery, prickled green
That shone and stang, lifting above our heads
In delicate arched bowers of flowers
Misty and dew-lost, spun out by weary stars
Woven in Heaven beside the angels' cloaks
And spat and stung with the sting of magic Hell,
Oh I knew you well, once;
There were no swans then.

Long-legged as a stork, clip-footed, high,
Clip-footed, lifting high—oh God, the swan
Was here, is gone and I cannot raise
My heavy body like hers and easily fly.

Swans are wild magnificent creatures
Born and cherished from dewdrops into
Ugly pearl-shaped goslings, beating like an oyster
Safe and coolly staring from his hole,
Could they too be grains of sand
Flown in from some deserted desert land
To sail and sail away? How does one
Get to become a swan? In a land
Like ours, it's easier to be a grain of sand.

The poet holds his pen like the swan its feather
Each loose, each clutching, one natural one not,
One flying one not.
Neither ever moves together.

My lover, my swan, you hold back from me
Like a wild madman, giving the black of your eyes
For wings and your wrinkled hands
As a sacrifice for the ice I eat
To have and become you. Fly, fly
And let me fly with you, I will give you
Earth and devils beating white and shining by lakes,
I will set fire to the earth with the bald dripping
Candle of sun for your sweet darling sake,
And these candles, these feathers, dripping round me, beating
Harsh in my head as I'm greeting and greeting,
Remind me of swans and their false gentle play
And the swans, the swans that will never fly away.

I searched for you in black forests
And caught the tuft of a ghost-spun feather
Melting into dew beside the wintry cold hard weather;
I found you there at one
With a dead swan.

These misty rays that crystallise out of the moon
Beware and betray my love, I see you hanging
Neatly balanced on the edge of this silver spoon
That wipes the night with the care of a fastidious dove,
I see the swans that line your neck with their beaks
And peck you, rising yet, their wings in a silver starry net
That trapped the stars and patched out the holes in the sky.

Swan, swan, swan
Flying low, flying high,
Flying cool, flying by,
And the frost in your eye
Hurts my love and I
And my love goes by
To the lake with a sigh
And I sit by the marble
And start to cry.

Let me draw you a picture of a swan:
Two beaks, one silent wing, one large
And open mouth, two wings, a silent flight
Of passing blackbirds, loosened in the sky,
The flattened grey shadow of mice
And man, perched high on buildings
Trying to fly, trying to sing,
Three beaks, one eye, three teeth, one wing.

Born as a swan and trapped into death
And her misty tempting fingers
Rising into ripped-out wings and shrouds
I hear the faint swans crying loud
And I stood and cried
And walked across to the other side.

Swans are broken and lonely,
Strange in white purity,
Revealing the mirror of the river into lines,
Making shiver all the lovers walking by
With the loveliness of their eye
And their cold, cold, hard, silver wings.

Love pulls white strings on her chariot
Drawn by swans and followed by death,
I follow dreaming through the empty sweet dawn
Laden with roses, chequered with colours,
I see the light rise in her eye,
I feel her fly and the wind fly
And I fly and sigh for I cannot fly.

My darling, do not trap me like the swan I saw netted
Who struggled and sweated with a great broken wing
Torn free, for I am me
And will not stand the strain of this false deluding pain
You force on me
And call love and shone
Like a dove
Not a swan.

Where are the rivers that flow swanless by?
I see the greedy look fall trickling out of your eye
And these harsh dry sunbeams, packing in stark red columns
Dry with dust, hard with hate, worshippers' dreams
Release the woman that flies and show the swan that seems.

What swan have you planted to grow like white thorns
Threshing within? The lilies weep not, nor spin,
But print and stand with silent feet outside
The ripe decked borders of the fields, and Summer passes,
I pass you and you will not yield—how can I say,
How can I hurt and left, yet gone
By the cooling curling contemptuous lip of a giant swan?

Swans' wings, swans' wings
Curling all together.
Love songs, children's songs
Calling in a feather.
Far away, the swans are playing
By a still sunset sea,
The wind is up, the tide is out,
The sun lies backless on the water's dream.

White and swan-faced agony
Lurks noble by most trembling lips of rivers,
Your eyes are no different,
Your hair like nests,
I could pluck you and wish for rest,
The forests are dark and lonely tonight
White with solitude, white with empty unusable wings,
And floating papers littered around obsess the mind
With blinding whirls of swans
Who fall and float like giants from the sky
Passing us by.

Resurrect a swan and kill a Christ
And line his throat with soft fur-mittened tails,
Swooping and shrieking, the swans are pale
Tonight, both they and I are mad.

I have dreams still of swans' flight
Lacing the clouds with still purple sound
And racing around on empty wings
And the world sings and stewing up and out men with a ladle
Rocks itself to sleep
A swan's cradle.

Belief and believe not.
Belief is too dangerous for these white heavy days;
I prefer graves and the mad swishing tails of swans
When crying, they know the agony
Of wings tightly forced to unfurl
Beneath a pale and straining world.

The wild swans breathe their last
And the shutters come tumbling down
Bathing in cold sleek white moonlight
Dropped in silver tears
From her large open eye that shadows the covering sun,
Oh leave me and fail in agony,
Shoot me here, let me feel the metal gun
And its soft metallic stroke on my wild white wing.

L'AUBE SPIRITUELLE   ▽

When white-pink dawns throb over busy women,
Happy men gnawing in ecstatic selfpride,
It hangs in its sheets accusations of broken
And sleeping angel bodies lying side by side,

These empty-faced skies in navy clear blue
Lie for the dreaming and those who feel pain,
Gape and reject with their darling 'I'll miss you',
Shudder like Goddesses pale and restrained.

Under the smoky ruined passions still thrusting
I remember more white and more clear and more care
From the open eyes of the mirror that dusting
Itself mirrors us with its silent cool stare.

The sun paints black all the candles' foul whispering
And rises, achieved, from its ghostly pale bed,
Its sound is clear, its light is still wisping
And under its shadows remain still the scandals
And under its shadows is hanging its head.

White and cold, faintly long as a pouring candle
Streaming with light, she creeps behind darkened doors,
Hiding the garlanded terrors she wears and knows
Constantly—dully-lit and hidden as the misting soil
That clings around a darkest red rose. A darling torture
Catches her soul in fires, true and tawny, she smokes
Beneath calmly smiling breath of a hellish sky, long and blue,
Carriaging in purples and gay, she marries and bend
Splits in a silver fork like the toes and arms of a weeping
Willow who lowers her soft and often sullen tears
Beyond into sinking grey—I loved you, darkness and white
Like a child that skipped with sunshine like rope
And wound the light around her throat in a
Glittering strangled necklace—killed with pearls
And eaten, she dies, to speak in kind and murmurs
Casual as waves, beating against a silent wall
Calling like the pink lips of a hasty undressed dawn
For the silvery satisfied comforts of the caring
Repetitive sun. Ah, Malfi, you fell like a flower
Pulled-out, uprooted, as great, as strong, as torn
As a huge and brilliant country, towering in gems
And scattered with silver broken lights. You,
Sweetest of all illusions, best of beauties
Ever frailed and broken by a light-tongued wind,
Came running with a rope, your rope, to thread helpless between
Your silent and famous loveliness, the quiet heart
And sleeping feathers of flying flung-out light you might have been.

▽

Time sinks with grace; losing ourselves in the pearl
Of Time and Time's disgrace, we sink and land
In baffled loneliness stuck on the sand
Of fervoured hair and faint-hearted freckled face.

(Based on the Stepdaughter in Pirandello's *Six Characters in Search of an Author*.)

Piano...piano...I told you piano that last part,
Well here I am, here I am, you're in the shadows,
You're in the blackness and I'm in the light, I'm the poet,
You're sitting, settling, waiting to gorge on a poetic feast,
That's not just poetry, not just muddy plain settled
Freckled unfriendly face of poetry, but drama too,
Theatre, action—packed and vivid—the poet speaks,
The poet moves, the poet acts and dances like the music,
See, see, one leg, one leg, one arm, one arm,
And suddenly a pose, a line that rhymes
And suddenly not prose but a poem and a dance
Drawn from the lines of conscience still beating,
The heart that doesn't stop but waits fixed for its moment
Of fine arrest...a cardiac arrest...a pose...a poem.
To you not real, the wind ruffles through the hay,
You gather the fine lace of your thoughts together
And concentrate on speaking, but, to me, here is a fence
And here is a line I draw against the fence,
A fine line, a black line that moves and shapes
And traces itself out to form a shadow, not of reality, not of life,
But crudity and darkness and death, see how the line moves,
And is joined in hateful hideous beating dramas by other lines,
An arm, a mother, a leg, a father, two breasts,
There's nothing there, no heart that beats, no legs that stretch,
Just the fine black lines of a ticking tragedy
Waiting outside stage-doors to be broken,
Here's my mother, look how she bends in the light,
She's grieving for me, her hair's dark too,
My father's dark and balding, see him come,
Wasting in, waltzing, he doesn't know me, he doesn't know,
No feelings, no feelings, it doesn't matter, it's a poem,
See him bend over her, then me, face full of distrust
And hatred, see us kiss, another comes, a little brother
Playing flowers in the stream, a little sister
Riding tricycles, playing, playing, the poet speaks,
It's all a play, it's all a fantastic flower-starred dream
Of roses and moonlight fucking together

On the eyelash of a silver world
That blinks and it's a pearl,
Listen, listen, see them, here, see the shadows
Glistening, listening, like you are shadows,
You glisten, you listen, condemn and despise,
Dislike and reprise, it's all right, we're a poem,
Let's poeticise together...I'm tired now,
I'm tired now...I want to sleep...but shadows,
Shadows rise from the dark deep hell of seats sleeping
Beyond, in front of me, seats like yourselves,
Listening to poems, clapping at drama, loving
Music's subtler tragedies, listen to me,
Listen to me please now, I want to sleep,
My mother's crying, she's shaking her head,
My father smiles, he kisses her instead,
My brother writes me letters, my sister
Hopes I won't get better...I'm tired...I'm tired now...
Oh God, I want to sleep...
Let me...[Takes pills]...let me...let me...
I will, I will, I will, see them walking, see the shadows
Walking, walking, like you will walk in grey mourning
Silently round a grave...oh God, I'm tired...yawn,
Yawn...silently round a grave...poets tread deep
In ideas and passions, yet never lift their heads
Above your seats, are you sitting there impassioned
Simply waiting for me to sleep, must I say to you,
Must I create, must I dream, must I deep, deep,
Deeply relate creatively to you, like this, watch:
    The grey thistles wandering above the torn and thunderous sky,
    The storm bends down on the hideous pity that's stolen its
                          /watchful cracking eye,
    Flying down the river, see the poetry fly
    Under the blue mane of a savage sky.
Must I see you, must I say this, before I sleep,
Such savagery never existed...not one to a...young
Must I say, it steals, it steals, must
I reel and reel of roses, moons and midnight,
Must I kneel with prayerful metered supplication,
Must I feel, oh Christ, how must I feel before you see it's real,
It's simply nothing else but real?

There are no shadows in this drama,
There are no poets in this procession,
There's just a death, a sleep, obsession,
That challenges and chimes and blinds through your minds,
Your minds, not mine,
    Four grey shadows walking round a coffin,
    Four grey shadows walking round a coffin,
    Swallow and swallow and swallow
    It's your deaths not mine,
    It's real, it's real
    And now I am going to sleep.

∇

Each single lightning step that cuts across the millions of a star
Forks me bewildered; fantastic passions, lovely lies
And sliding gushing dreams; from these deep broodings
Great philosophies are formed that beckon with the Night
And a single bloody hand towards the white signpost,
Death, where every pedlar passes, flirting ribbons,
Led white-cheeked in panting colours down beneath stone crosses
Suitcased and timbered at last. The far and green
Murmurings of trees recall graves and building snows,
The paleness of the muffled shroud that clings
In white and donkey hair around the old man's skull.

PARFUM EXOTIQUE ▽

Under the rich lushness of Beauty's disgrace
I see her small red painted lips
That purse up tight and pop,
Her wiles like small ripe greedy plums
Burst into smiles.

Oh your breasts and your valleys are luscious and happy,
The white folds of your hair is fragrant and free
And under the solid chiming sun
I feel your savoury fingers languorously reach for me.

The lazy sullen island where you live
Beneath the sky in silent frankness,
Smelling only you and led by you
I trap the golden feathers of the sky,
I wail and lie bereaved beneath the waves
That flutter past their sad silent bodies tilted high.

Oh the perfume of life you wear is rich
And heady, small in my ship
Beneath you I'll float,
And lie dead in your silent, sea-starry ditch.

▽

Hands bitter and clenching burn their fists
In bitter fight with Time. Across the evening sky
Birds rise startled to their clear and subtle flocks.
Far behind Winter's wrinkled nose, they spread
And gather in blankets of vivid blacks
Lurking in covered warmth above the spiked
And ribcaged brittle lines of trees.

Brief, brief and bright as a shorn-off silver candle
Through the reaching pouring swirls of water,
Sank Nora, like a bird—her hair of thickly coarsened rope
Knotted with streaking streaming green—that glittered like corpses'
                     /legs through the falling water.
Ah, the faint far hooves of easy-speaking horses
Neighing through the water's bright white coats,
They foam and prance and leap in
Curling, curving bubbles to the shore. And Kathleen sings, of
                     /cakes unruined,
Waterheads that splinter, undissolving, into beaded strings of beauty,
Silvery chained round a glass that mirrors dead men's faces,
Pearls, wide and bright and cool as skull,
Lurk falling through the water. Maurya's hair,
And Kathleen's spinning, Nora's stranded
Loveliness rush together in silken watery folds that drip,
Pouring in loveliness round the silent, strewn and sea-flowered
                     /coffin. Horses calling in the distance.

▽

How does Life, finally wasted, meet us here
And how are we, penguins, on the edge of a coal-black shore
Arriving distanced, flapping our flippers like wings
And shrieking ugly and cruel for love. Shoot all penguins,
Kill Nature with her own force, that's the way
To drag in hideous Night and save us all from pretty pretentious Day.

Time's silken steps mount the ladder and pause
At the top, to deck in fantastic gleams
Around the stars, they fail and startled cause
The huge rocking of the night of the Universe's dreams,
And love, — in a nightie, shy and cold and awake,
Waits blue-handed by the open window and rain
And watches the mice with frost-topped heads as they make
Their quivering paths across the wooden floor in pain
And memories of dark, deep cats rising like midnight beyond
And searching with concrete steel tooths, with a flare,
For these quick grey shadows vanished and frightened and fond
And clutching themselves with the suddenness of their scare,
    And love, in her nightie and white, drifts out to the cold
    Like a dream and waits there until she is old.

All of the nightmare turns inside out and black
As the Universe reverses itself and scattered turns
Her shaved head scaring and crying alas and alack
Bring out the knives, there is something that I must burn,
Something is red and turning and small and pleads like a bee
In the Summer's fanciful air, playing like pipers,
Arousing itself with me and shifting in seeds
That glow in white opium startles like a flipper
For sex and glory at once, count numbers now,
Here's the Night, old and weird and blind,
Count murder now dragging a sour old sow
With wisdom looking out from the eyes of her mind,
    Oh Philosophy's a wretch and aching crutch
    Reduced and so are we. Nonesuch! Nonesuch!

He strolled around all the grey leaves
All grey and loose in the stringing olives
And stuffed a dusty head
Deep between their deep heat.

So now what? Finish? Blindness
Leaves as the leaves are falling, leaving
I, what is it then I must say to you
To find you when I cannot, oh blind, blind.

Endless unfinishings, neither here nor
Elsewhere where they sit, this stone
Is snow-hard and shallow, from where did it fall?
To which trees do we belong?

Flaked and wasted with age, geared to
Solitary, trained to your lap,
Where are you, faint exister
Filled with quiet shamefulness...?

The waves flow, the waves flow,
The sea is green...
Your hand shakes,
You are not
You are not
Where do you go?

And finally in comes an angel,
The scene—why, by the way, did she come,
I saw Night running with a knife
Through the trees' shocked branches,
Men move too in dreams with knives,
Why angels?

Only Night runs carrying knives
With friends, smiling hundreds come
Sleeping like black dogs, peeing on stones
In the dim mourning of many thousands
Bleaking by seas...
And then comes morning.

Angels walk not late at night
Praying to these, nights in their torn black robes
Finally stop growing, those who lose
Are lossless and lie dressed by flying angels
Beaten out by women, drawn by men,
Let them too settle, sleep, pray
Here waiting by grey leaves.

ANTIGONE'S LAMENT ▽

Dead and unmarried I walk silent along the green leaves
Curling and stretching beyond a dead wet Paradise—bloody brides
Call swooning in white mutters through the rosy dewdropped tears
/of Dawn
Who greets me smiling, dropping a golden veil to shed
In glittering trembles its life over me in sweet and delicate tumbles;
City, city and brothers strong in bruising life, they fall like
/brownly withered leaves
In tumbling windswept graves around my feet, I trap the storm
And lie here crying alone in the damp grass where the gods walk,
Perishing under their silver feet and dripping with tears,
Naked pansies stain my cheeks with bloodlet blushes, shameless
And a whore I lie, skirts upturned and virginal, blank-faced
Hopeful beside the river of death, the waters are calling
Of oblivious sleep, Death winds over me, a breezing crow
Whose eyes are warm and black, a brother's eyes are falling
In wizened gladness in me, Antigone, silent and sure, a baby to
/the grave.

△

(Written to be performed to an extract from Debussy's *La Mer*—the end of the
Second Movement and the beginning of the Third—and, from line 11, to 'The
Dance of the Sugar-Plum Fairy' from Tchaikovsky's *Nutcracker Suite*.)

Orange. . .autumn. . .tints of violet,
Orange. . .autumn. . .tints of violet,

Life's velvet bloomers streaking down
In hints of lace and tints of wet

Black. White.

Orange. . .autumn. . .tints of violet

I could tell you love me madly
So gladly. My puppet on a string.

What's this? Where are you going?

What's this? And what are you?

One light. . .two lights. . .three lights. . .four lights,
Candles burning in a misty morning.

There, in the gloom, I see a stranger talking,
Lies are in his eyes, and his knees are stroked with green,

Walking by the river on a Sunday morning,
Petals twinkling falling from a mad and muddy stream.

Is he sleeping? Shall I call him? Floating from the garden?
King of water lilies shining from his eyes and flame.
He's wrapped in a green cloak, eyes full of marigolds,
Can he see me, is he listening for the rain?
And. . .and. . .and. . .
Cold winds,
Love sings
Like a bird who's strangled when she's heard,
High tides,
Love rides
And sounds, and drowns, and found and drowned
And gallops as she pale-faced looks, sees Death is by her side.

Yellow tints of autumn flowers
Decking down in lilac bowers.

Listen to the clock,
Listen to its tock,
Listen 'cause he's looking,
'Cause he's looking at my face,
Has he seen the bird?
Is it lies he heard?
Oh love you're singing sweetly
But you're beating round my face.

Come and take me darling,
Here I'm waiting in the garden,
Lay your long green eyes upon me like those lilies shine with rain,

Fly us free together, fly us hawks in golden weather,
Oh Christ, this green-eyed bird pecks out my eyes with pain.

▽

Oh love, spit out this food that is not you
Nor yet is me; in lovely slender glows
I saw the moon from straws build up refuse
And dirtying sink its spots beneath its nose.
I saw a smile that started like a horse
Then, bolting, leaped and stretched beyond its teeth,
And grossly leaping, sprang outside its course,
And galloped wayward on the face-lit heath,
The moon lurched out, the smile lurched in, we find
In every grosser spirit, grosser whole
That soft-diseased breeds quickly through the mind
And rots the face and perishes the soul,
   And every Universe that hurts my heart
   I loathe this whole, and long for only part.

Jealousy creams and curdles the night
Setting the milk like mice alight
And leaving the stars ajar, had we fought
Ever against it, we'd never know now
Who we are.

Blue, gold, red, intered,
A space and rockets gold
Intertwined, a mad and noisy scene,
The slam of a parlour door,
Mary's gone, my love is here,
That damned bell rings again,
Call the police, release me
From my pain. Had you not
Murdered, no-one could have come
In forcible entries, finding you dead
Clasping a vivid Danger road sign,
Brilliant crazy red and white,
Found you asleep in pyjamas
At eleven and still in bed.

How bitter Winter wreathes her hair with winds
And nails in her hair, the blood runs red and thin
Over the narrow streets, love cries out at harshness
In a turban and petrified weeps as the sun drops her gown
In rainbow-shimmered glory at her feet, let the sun rise,
Let the earth set, the green and bitterness felt here
Will rise in Winter's Spring and ice and set hard again for another
/year.